It's More Than Just a Prayer

Matthew L. Adrianson

In the summer of 2022, God birthed a desire in me to put into words the Christian faith backed up by scripture. Originally, I thought of this as a personal test; little did I know God's intentions were much greater. Knowing something is one thing, but being able to articulate those thoughts and ideas can be more challenging. Just because you know something doesn't mean you can demonstrate it or communicate it. I know from teaching music over the years that it can take presenting the same information multiple ways before finally connecting with a student.

Being able to define what you believe and why you believe it is important. Making sure those beliefs line up with what God has said through His Word concerning salvation, being born again, submitting to the Lordship of Jesus Christ, and what the life of a believer looks like is essential. We need to look at the Bible as a whole, read, study, pray, and seek the Holy Spirit to lead us into all truth.

God has revealed Himself, His nature, His plan, and His will in the Bible. God makes things that are important to illuminate on the pages of scripture for those who seek Him and read His Word.

Pray and ask God to let His will be done in your life, no matter what that might be. Once you know God's love for you, His character, and His faithfulness, it will become easier to put all your trust in Him.

Proverbs 3:5-6 NASB *"Trust in the LORD with all your heart and do not lean on your own understanding.⁶ In all your ways acknowledge Him, and He will make your paths straight."*

Anyone who's come to God in faith and repentance will have a testimony. A testimony will get a conversation started, but then what? If we are going to be an effective witness, we need to spend time in God's Word and be led by the Holy Spirit.

God instructs believers to share their faith and to be ready to give an account for what they believe.

1 Peter 3:15 NASB *"but sanctify Christ as Lord in your hearts, always being ready to make a defense to everyone who asks you to give an account for the hope that is in you, but with gentleness and respect."*

Sharing your faith is important, even if it seems intimidating. Scripture even states that someone has to say something for the message to be heard.

Romans 10:14 NASB *"How then are they to call on Him in whom they have not believed? How are they to believe in Him whom they have not heard? And how are they to hear without a preacher?"*

Believers are also called ambassadors in

2 Corinthians 5:20. An ambassador is someone who represents someone else, and in this case, introduces them to God.

2 Corinthians 5:20 NASB *"Therefore, we are ambassadors for Christ, as though God were making an appeal through us; we beg you on behalf of Christ, be reconciled to God."*

My prayer is that this short book will help those who don't know Jesus discover God's love for them and come to salvation through faith.

For those who have prayed a prayer of faith yet lack understanding, a firm foundation will be established. For some to realize that God desires to have a one-on-one personal relationship with them. For others who struggle to share their faith, find within the pages of this book enough scripture, knowledge, and wisdom to help them start stepping out and be a witness.

God has so much in store for those who fully commit and choose to trust Him. Don't hold back any part of your life and watch what God will do.

CONTENTS

INTRODUCTION

Embracing who Jesus Christ is for yourself—the Son of God, God the Son, Lord, Savior, and Messiah—is the most important thing you could ever do. A combination of putting your trust in what Jesus has accomplished through the cross and confessing what you believe sets everything into motion. This act of faith begins your spiritual journey and relationship with God.

Romans 10:9–10 NASB *"That if you confess with your mouth Jesus as Lord and believe in your heart that God raised Him from the dead, you will be saved; ¹⁰for with the heart a person believes, resulting in righteousness, and with the mouth he confesses, resulting in salvation."*

Matthew 10:32 AMP *"Therefore, the one who confesses and acknowledges Me before men as Lord and Savior, affirming a state of oneness with Me, that one I will also confess and acknowledge before My Father who is in heaven."*

Maybe you heard a sermon, or someone shared with you that Jesus died on the cross to pay the price for your sin.

Romans 6:23 NASB *"For the wages of sin is death, but the gracious gift of God is eternal life in Christ Jesus our Lord."*

Know that this gift is only applied to you and activated in you through faith and confession.

If you acted on the message of salvation, it was because what you heard stirred something up inside you. The truth you heard was confirmed in your spirit by the Holy Spirit. Then you not only heard the truth, but you "took action"—you did something with it.

Accepting God's gracious gift includes these components:

- Repenting (changing what you think about Jesus and sin)
- Confessing and turning from your sin
- Putting your faith in the death and resurrection of Jesus (Believing His sacrifice pays the debt owed for your sin)
- Confessing Jesus as your Lord (surrendering your will to God)

Jesus' blood covers your sin, paying your debt in full once you accept what Jesus did for you personally. Your faith and confession of Jesus as Lord results in Jesus becoming your savior, the forgiveness of your sin, and a reconciliation between you and God. At this point, you are saved by grace through faith, and the Spirit of the living God will come and live inside you. Jesus described this as being born again.

John 3:6-7 NASB *"That which has been born of the flesh is flesh, and that which has been born of the Spirit is spirit. [7]Do not be amazed that I said to you, 'You must be born again.'"*

2 Corinthians 5:17 NASB *"Therefore if anyone is in Christ, this person is a new creation; the old things passed away; behold, new things have come."*

Romans 8:11 NASB *"But if the Spirit of Him who raised Jesus from the dead dwells in you, He who raised Christ Jesus from the dead will also give life to your mortal bodies through His Spirit who dwells in you."*

It is a spiritual birth, transforming you from the kingdom of this world into God's kingdom.

Colossians 1:13 NASB *"For He rescued us from the domain of darkness and transferred us to the kingdom of His beloved Son."*

It's important to note that it's more than just a prayer you pray, but putting your faith in God for salvation includes repentance and surrendering your will to God. This surrender is a submission to the Lordship of Jesus Christ, which is ongoing and includes living according to the teachings of Jesus.

Matthew 28:20 NASB *"teaching them to follow all that I commanded you; and behold, I am with you always, to the end of the age."*

Embracing who Jesus Christ is for yourself —the Son of God, God the Son, Lord, Savior, and Messiah— is the most important thing you could ever do.

YOUR SEED

Faith is like a seed planted in your heart (innermost being) and has certain needs to take root and grow.

1 Peter 1:23 NASB *"For you have been born again not of seed, which is perishable, but imperishable, that is, through the living and enduring word of God."*

Protecting your seed and doing things that will help it grow, is as important as the seed being planted in the first place. Spending time with God in prayer, reading His Word, and being in fellowship with other believers will protect your seed and help it grow.

John 15:4 NASB *"Remain in Me, and I in you. Just as the branch cannot bear fruit of itself but must remain in the vine, so neither can you unless you remain in Me."*

Romans 12:2 NIV *"Do not conform to the pattern of this world but be transformed by the renewing of your mind. Then you will be able to test and approve what God's will is—his good, pleasing, and perfect will."*

Our minds are transformed as we read the Word of God and spend time in prayer. Also, spending time with other believers reinforces the truth you know and are learning as you share testimonies and fellowship.

Proverbs 27:17 NASB *"As iron sharpens iron, so one person sharpens another."*

There are things that will try to steal your seed, like Satan, persecution, anxiety, the cares and concerns of this world, and the deceitfulness of wealth. That is why it is important to have confidence in what you believe, why you believe it, and have scripture as your foundation. As you apply what Jesus taught to your everyday life, there will be evidence of it taking root and growing.

Concerning the things that would try and steal or destroy your seed, it is important to recognize who is for you and who is against you.

1 John 4:4 AMP *"Little children (believers, dear ones), you are of God, and you belong to Him and have [already] overcome them [the agents of the antichrist]; because He who is in you is greater than he (Satan) who is in the world [of sinful mankind.]"*

Ephesians 6:12 NIV *"For our struggle is not against flesh and blood, but against the rulers, against the authorities, against the powers of this dark world and against the spiritual forces of evil in the heavenly realms."*

Jesus uses an illustration to explain what happens when the Word of God is preached. He tells it as a parable which can appear to hide the truth, but it reveals the truth to those seeking it. After telling the parable to the crowd, He goes on to explain its meaning to His disciples. The seed is the message of salvation, and the soil is a person's heart. Here is what Jesus said to His disciples:

Matthew 13:18–23 NASB *"Listen then to the parable of the sower.¹⁹When anyone hears the word of the kingdom and does not understand it, the evil one comes and snatches away what has been sown in his heart. This is the one sown with seed beside the road.²⁰The one sown with seed on the rocky places, this is the one who hears the word and immediately receives it with joy.²¹yet he has no firm root in himself, but is only temporary, and when affliction or persecution occurs because of the word, immediately he falls away.²²And the one sown with seed among the thorns, this is the one who hears the word, and the anxiety of the world and the deceitfulness of wealth choke the word, and it becomes unfruitful.²³But the one sown with seed on the good soil, this is the one who hears the word and understands it, who indeed bears fruit and produces, some a hundred, some sixty, and some thirty times as much."*

Good soil includes repentance, confession, turning from your sin; faith in the death and resurrection of Jesus; and confessing Jesus as Lord. Seed sown in good soil will result in a changed life.

Notice how some believe yet fall away. That is why protecting your seed and doing things to help it grow are vital. Jesus used the analogy of bearing fruit to say there will be positive evidence of a seed sown in good soil. This is not to say that we earn salvation; salvation is a gift.

> Protecting your seed and doing things that will help it grow, is as important as the seed being planted in the first place.

READ THE ROADMAP

Imagine a race. One day, you heard about a race, and you were invited to participate. They start out telling you it's a marathon, not a sprint. They tell you that it's not going to be easy but that if you participate, you won't regret it, and your reward will be worth whatever effort is given to get to the finish line. After hearing enough details about the race, you decide to participate.

Someone shows you where to register, explains the parameters and provides a roadmap showing the path from start to finish. Then you hear someone say, "On your mark, get set, go!"

To compare this with coming to God for salvation, the registration part is when you repent and put your faith in Jesus. The roadmap for the race is God's Word. God provided the roadmap because He knew we needed one. If you don't know much about God or what the Bible says yet, don't worry. We are saved by grace through faith and not by how much we know.

Reading the Bible is necessary to gain wisdom, knowledge, and direction. Reading God's Word daily will help you stay on the right path.

If you've never read the Bible or it's been a while, I suggest reading the Gospel of John, Acts, Romans, and Colossians. Read a chapter a day, then write out what you think God is saying in each chapter. Then, personalize it, try to make it into a prayer, and do it out loud. You will be amazed at what this can do for your understanding of Scripture and your relationship with God.

GOD'S WORD

The Bible is the inspired Word of God.

2 Timothy 3:16 NASB *"All Scripture is inspired by God and beneficial for teaching, for rebuke, for correction, for training in righteousness."*

Romans 15:4 NASB *"For whatever was written in earlier times was written for our instruction, so that through perseverance and the encouragement of the Scriptures we might have hope."*

2 Peter 1:20–21 NASB *"But know this first of all, that no prophecy of Scripture becomes a matter of someone's own interpretation,[21] for no prophecy was ever made by an act of human will, but men moved by the Holy Spirit spoke from God."*

The Bible is a very long book, and some say, "I've read the Bible, but I don't really understand it." It's actually broken up between the Old Testament and the New Testament—66 books in all. There are thought to be around 40 authors; all inspired by the Holy Spirit. The Bible was penned over approximately 1500 years. The Old Testament documents the covenants God made with Adam, Noah, Abraham, Moses, and David. In the New Testament God established a new covenant that extends to "all who believe" through the death and resurrection of Jesus. All 66 books woven together tell the story of how God loves us and provided a way of reconciliation back to Himself by grace through faith.

John 3:16 NASB *"For God so loved the world, that He gave His only Son, so that everyone who believes in Him will not perish but have eternal life."*

People go to Bible school, study the Bible, and get degrees in it. After spending years studying, they can still read it again and again and learn something new. The Bible is described as being alive and active.

Hebrews 4:12 NIV *"For the word of God is alive and active. Sharper than any double-edged sword, it penetrates even to dividing soul and spirit, joints, and marrow; it judges the thoughts and attitudes of the heart."*

Jesus is the Word of God incarnate (in the flesh).

John 1:1 NIV *"In the beginning was the Word, and the Word was with God, and the Word was God."*

John 1:14 NIV *"The Word became flesh and made his dwelling among us. We have seen his glory, the glory of the one and only Son, who came from the Father, full of grace and truth."*

The Bible is what feeds our spirit, and it's important not to starve it.

Matthew 4:4 NIV *"Jesus answered, 'It is written: 'Man shall not live on bread alone, but on every word that comes from the mouth of God.'"*

The Old Testament was originally written in Hebrew, and the New Testament was originally written in Greek.

You can really get into long studies on how the original text was translated into English. You can study what the original Greek and Hebrew words were and how that can add more understanding and meaning to every scripture. The goal of this book, however, is not to dive into Greek and Hebrew language studies but to provide an overview of what God's Word says about salvation and living a life as a believer.

I will take you on a journey through some highlights of the Bible to give you a foundation for your walk with God. This will include some history, starting with the creation story, the death and resurrection of Jesus, the second coming of Jesus, and some of what the Bible says about judgment and the end of days.

There's so much that could be said, but the bulk of what I'm sharing will be scripture, God's Word, so that it will have power to work in your life. God's Word, if activated, will transform your mind, place you, and keep you on the right path.

> All 66 books woven together tell the story of how God loves us and provided a way of reconciliation back to Himself by grace through faith.

A COVENANT RELATIONSHIP

You may have prayed a prayer in a church service or by yourself to personally accept what Jesus did on the cross as payment for your sin. You believe He took your place, died on your behalf, and that God the Father raised Him from the dead. You asked God to forgive you for your sin. You repented and confessed Jesus as your Lord.

Romans 10:9–10 NASB *"that if you confess with your mouth Jesus as Lord and believe in your heart that God raised Him from the dead, you will be saved; [10] for with the heart a person believes, resulting in righteousness, and with the mouth he confesses, resulting in salvation."*

The question you might be asking yourself is, "What did I actually do?" Or "What does this mean for my life in practical terms?"

You entered into a covenant relationship with Almighty God just in the same way that a man and a woman go before a pastor or a judge and make marriage vows.

The noun tense of the Greek word for covenant is diathéké. Strong's Concordance says, "In simple terms, a covenant means a testament or will. In proper usage, a set of agreements having complete terms determined by the initiating party that is also fully affirmed by the one entering the agreement."

Covenants define obligations and commitments, but they are different from a contract because they are relational and personal. Covenants can be broken, but in this case, God promises never to leave us or forsake us (Hebrews 13:5–6).

We also need to make sure we are staying in covenant with God. In a human marriage, if the husband or wife steps out of their covenant to be with someone else, we would call that adultery or a breach of that covenant. Because we love God, we should honor our covenant with Him and not cheat on Him.

Jesus laid the foundation when He said the greatest commandment was to love the Lord your God with all your heart, soul, mind, and strength (Mark 12:30). Know that our being able to love God is only possible because God first loved us (John 3:16). Reading this as a command seems odd, but God only requires of us what He has already given to us regarding love.

It's worth defining love from God's Word.

1 Corinthians 13:4–7 NASB *"Love is patient, love is kind, it is not jealous; love does not brag, it is not arrogant,⁵ It does not act disgracefully, it does not seek its own benefit; it is not provoked, does not keep an account of a wrong suffered,⁶ it does not rejoice in unrighteousness, but rejoices with the truth; ⁷ it keeps every confidence, it believes all things, hopes all things, endures all things."*

Bottom line: If you love your earthly spouse, you won't cheat on them. We can cheat on God by doing things that offend or grieve Him. Focus on loving God, and you will see correct behavior follow.

It's really a challenge for everyone, including myself, to evaluate if we truly love God with all our heart, soul, mind, and strength, and if we are living our lives in a way that demonstrates that love? If not, thankfully, God has patience beyond ours, and we can pray that God helps us, repent, and keep trying (1 John 1:9).

Day by day, we are transformed into the likeness of Jesus if we submit ourselves to the process. The Holy Spirit will work in us and through us until one day, we will see Jesus face-to-face.

2 Corinthians 3:18 NASB *"But we all, with unveiled faces, looking as in a mirror at the glory of the Lord, are being transformed into the same image from glory to glory, just as from the Lord, the Spirit."*

Our bodies are even called "the temple of the Holy Spirit." God's Spirit comes to dwell (live) in us, when we repent and confess Jesus as our Lord.

1 Corinthians 6:19 AMP *"Do you not know that your body is a temple of the Holy Spirit who is within you, whom you have [received as a gift] from God, and that you are not your own [property]?"*

Relationships take time and effort. We are better for them when we make the proper investment. You wouldn't get married here on earth and then, after saying your vows, leave the church in separate cars and go separate ways. God wants to spend time with you. You need to spend time with God. The church is even called the Bride of Christ.

2 Corinthians 11:2 NLT *"For I am jealous for you with the jealousy of God himself. I promised you as a pure bride to one husband—Christ."*

Ephesians 5:27 NLT *"He did this to present her to himself as a glorious church without a spot or wrinkle or any other blemish. Instead, she will be holy and without fault."*

The ultimate purpose of Jesus dying on your behalf was to restore the relationship between you and God.

Colossians 1:20 NASB *"and through Him to reconcile all things to Himself, whether things on earth or things in heaven, having made peace through the blood of His cross."*

Just as the Scripture says, when a man and a woman are married, the two become one (Matthew 19:5); the same is true when you make this covenant relationship with God.

1 Corinthians 6:17 AMP *"But the one who is united and joined to the Lord is one spirit with Him."*

Romans 6:5 AMP *"For if we have become one with Him [permanently united] in the likeness of His death, we will also certainly be [one with Him and share fully] in the likeness of His resurrection."*

> This is incredible that God, the creator of the universe, wants to have a personal relationship and spend time with us.

WHAT IS REPENTING?

What does it mean to repent? The Greek word used for "repent" in Acts 2:38 is metanoeó. Strong's Concordance defines metanoeó as "to change one's mind or purpose." Strong's goes on to say, "I repent, change my mind, change the inner man (particularly with reference to acceptance of the will of God), repent."

Acts 2:38 NIV *"Peter replied, "Repent and be baptized, every one of you, in the name of Jesus Christ for the forgiveness of your sins. And you will receive the gift of the Holy Spirit."*

Repenting is changing from one way of thinking and behaving to something different. Another way to say it is to stop doing one thing and start doing something else. The application of Acts 2:38 is to turn from a life of sin, of being your own god, or serving the god of this world (Satan) to God. Repenting boils down to changing the way you think about Jesus and sin. When Jesus was on earth, one of the foremost things He was saying was that He was the Son of God, and most did not believe Him.

John 10:38 AMP *"But if I am doing them, even if you do not believe Me or have faith in Me, [at least] believe the works [that I do—admit that they are the works of God], so that you may know and keep on knowing [clearly—without any doubt] that the Father is in Me, and I am in the Father [that is, I am One with Him]."*

John 8:58 NASB Jesus said to them, *"Truly, truly I say to you, before Abraham was born, I am."*

The first step in repenting is believing differently about who Jesus is. Jesus is the Son of God, God the Son, the Messiah, the savior of the world, the lamb of God, and Jesus is Lord!

What does Lord mean? The Greek word used for Lord in Romans 10:9 is "kýrios," and the short definition is lord and master. In practical application, kýrios is, properly, a person exercising absolute ownership rights— lord (Lord)." The Bible even says we were bought with a price (1 Corinthians 6:20). To be bought implies that you become someone else's property. The reality is that God created you and loves you. He redeemed you with the blood of His Son, Jesus. The word redemption comes from the Greek word "apolutrósis," meaning a release effected by the payment of a ransom. In application, apolutrósis literally means "buying back from, re-purchasing (winning back) what was previously forfeited (lost)."

When you understand what God has for you is better than anything you could ever dream up, submitting to God's will isn't hard. Yet, our human nature leans toward wanting to be its own master. Think of this: A loving parent wants the best for their children. Parents do things with their children's best interest in mind. God the Father not only does everything with our best interest in mind but also with wisdom, love, power, and insight beyond what any earthly parent could ever do.

Then, concerning sin, it is to turn from a life of sin to God and His standard. You might ask, "What is sin?" Sin is anything that violates God's standard and/or nature.

The result of changing what you think about sin should result in a change in how you behave.

Romans 3:23 NASB *"for all have sinned and fall short of the glory of God."*

In God's Word, the Bible, God's standard is clearly stated. Most people have at least heard of the Ten Commandments. The Ten Commandments are found in the Old Testament in the book of Exodus, chapter 20, verses 3–17. I will paraphrase them:

- You shall have no other gods before me. (There is only one true living God, and we can only worship and serve Him.)
- You shall not have or make idols in any form, and you shall not bow down to them or worship them. (Idols are anything that we make more important than God. To worship in this context is not just to physically bow before; but it can also be submitting to something or someone's control or authority, looking to it for provision, or placing trust or faith in anything other than God concerning the things of God.)
- You shall not misuse the name of the Lord, your God. (God's name is holy and sacred and should only be used in honor and reverence. "LORD" in all capitols was translated from YHWH from the original Hebrew text. The Jews thought this proper name of God was so sacred that they would not even say it. Doing things in the name of Jesus that

are not of Jesus could also be considered taking the Lord's name in vain.)

- Remember the Sabbath day by keeping it holy. (The seventh day of the week, God said, was holy, meaning to rest and not work. In its original form, it was extreme, beyond what most understand or practice today. The Sabbath in the old covenant was Saturday, but in A.D. 325, the early church changed the day of rest to Sunday, calling it the Lord's Day. In the New Covenant, Paul talks about one day not being more sacred than another (Romans 14:5). We should dedicate our lives, honor God, and live right every day of the week because our bodies are now the temple of the Holy Spirit and God is with us all the time. With that said, God designed our bodies to need rest, so practicing a Sabbath day is wise and follows a pattern God established.)
- Honor your father and your mother. (Respect and obey your parents)
- You shall not murder.
- You shall not commit adultery. (Any sexual behavior or thoughts outside of the covenant of marriage fall under this command.)
- You shall not steal.
- You shall not give false testimony against your neighbor. (Lie about)
- You shall not covet anything that does not belong to you. (Be consumed with desire for)

Jewish law actually has 613 laws, and the point is that no one has ever been able to keep them except Jesus. Repenting includes changing from living a lifestyle that violates God's standard to living a lifestyle that follows God's standard. Some might say that the law is no longer valid, and that Jesus fulfilled the law. The fact is that Jesus fulfilled all the requirements of the law, and at the same time, the New Testament teaches us to live a pure life.

Matthew 5:17 NLT *"Don't misunderstand why I have come. I did not come to abolish the law of Moses or the writings of the prophets. No, I came to accomplish their purpose."*

1 Peter 1:16 NLT For the Scriptures say, *"You must be holy because I am holy."*

Jesus even adds more commandments and makes some of the original commandments more difficult to keep.

Matthew 5:28 NLT *"But I say, anyone who even looks at a woman with lust has already committed adultery with her in his heart."*

Luke 6:27–28 NASB *"But I say to you who hear, love your enemies, do good to those who hate you,*[28]*bless those who curse you, pray for those who are abusive to you."*

Anything Jesus said as an instruction is a new command and is the standard that we are supposed to live by. The topic that God's standard didn't go away could lead down a legalistic path, but my point is that repenting and living God's way is part of the journey. When questioned about the law, Jesus hung all of the law on these two commandments.

Mark 12:30–31 NLT *"And you must love the Lord your God with all your heart, all your soul, all your mind, and all your strength.³¹ The second is equally important: 'Love your neighbor as yourself.' No other commandment is greater than these."*

And further, when the Apostles accepted that even gentiles could be saved, these instructions were given to all the new gentile believers (a gentile is anyone who is not a Jew).

Acts 15:29 NASB *"That you abstain from things sacrificed to idols, from blood, from things strangled, and from acts of sexual immorality; if you keep yourselves free from such things, you will do well. Farewell."*

And then the crème de la crème statement Jesus made concerning sin is found in John chapter 8.

John 8:11 NLT "No, Lord," she said. And Jesus said, "Neither do I. Go and sin no more."

Remember, we cannot earn salvation. Salvation is a gift. Living holy is not about earning our salvation. We are saved by Grace through faith. Once we are saved, the Holy Spirit empowers us to live a holy life. We live holy because God is holy, and we are to be a reflection of Him. God comes to live inside us through the Holy Spirit to help us, to teach us, to guide us, and to comfort us. Remember grace doesn't give us a license to sin but an opportunity to repent and turn from it.

Galatians 6:7–8 NASB *"Do not be deceived, God is not mocked; for whatever a person sows, this he will also reap.[8] For the one who sows to his own flesh will reap destruction from the flesh, but the one who sows to the Spirit will reap eternal life from the Spirit."*

The covenant God established through Moses in the Old Testament was focused on laws, rules, and regulations, and was made with the children of Israel (Jews).

In the new covenant, for "all who believe", the focus shifts to love, not a list of dos and don'ts. However, the moral laws get restated in the New Testament to remind everyone that God still hates sin. Sin is still wrong, and sin was what broke the relationship between God and man.

Love does not try to do things that are offensive. The closer you get to God, the harder it will be to sin. God will help you and lead you into right behavior, not behavior that offends Him. This is why it is important to have an ongoing daily relationship with God. If you find yourself pulled into wrong thinking or behavior, repent, and ask God to help you. God wants you to succeed; He is for you and not against you.

Romans 8:14 NASB *"For all who are being led by the Spirit of God, these are sons and daughters of God."*

I want to restate that we are not saved by works or by following laws.

Romans 3:20 AMP *"For no person will be justified [freed of guilt and declared righteous] in His sight by [trying to do] the works of the Law. For through the Law we become conscious of sin [and the recognition of sin directs us toward repentance, but provides no remedy for sin]."*

There is no eternal moral scale where our good works are put on one side, and our sin is put on the other, and if the weight of our good works outweighs the weight of our sin, we get to go to heaven. No one is good enough in and of themselves. Everyone needs a savior. Everyone needs to have the payment of their sin paid for by the blood of Jesus.

Romans 3:23 NIV *"For all have sinned and fall short of the glory of God."*

Romans 6:23 NASB *"For the wages of sin is death, but the gracious gift of God is eternal life in Christ Jesus our Lord."*

Repenting is to turn from sin to God and boils down to changing the way you think about Jesus and sin.

THE BATTLE OF SIN

We are still humans and live in a fallen world. You might ask, "What if I do sin?"

1 John 1:9 NIV *"If we confess our sins, he is faithful and just and will forgive us our sins and purify us from all unrighteousness."*

1 John 2:1-2 NLT *"My dear children, I am writing this to you so that you will not sin. But if anyone does sin, we have an advocate who pleads our case before the Father. He is Jesus Christ, the one who is truly righteous.²He himself is the sacrifice that atones for our sins and not only our sins but the sins of all the world."*

Living a godly life can only be achieved "in Christ" and with the help of the Holy Spirit. You need God to empower you to live this way.

John 14:16–17 NASB *"I will ask the Father, and He will give you another Helper, so that He may be with you forever; ¹⁷the Helper is the Spirit of truth, whom the world cannot receive, because it does not see Him or know Him; but you know Him because He remains with you and will be in you."*

Ezekiel 36:27 AMP *"I will put my Spirit within you and cause you to walk in My statutes, and you will keep My ordinances and do them."*

Everything starts in our minds with how we think. Our mind is a battlefield. Even after we repent, confess, believe, and surrender; our flesh will want to fight against God's standard. This is why submitting to God, reading His Word, and being led by the Holy Spirit is so important.

Romans 12:2 NASB *"And do not be conformed to this world, but be transformed by the renewing of your mind, so that you may prove what the will of God is, that which is good and acceptable and perfect."*

Notice how Paul addresses the church. Paul always addresses the church as "saints," not sinners. This doesn't mean that believers are perfect, but our identity is no longer in our sin or in the world but in Christ. Christ is perfect, and we are made blameless in Him before God the Father. You will find strength in resisting sin when you have the mindset of being God's child and a saint. Those who remain identifing as sinners will find it harder to resist temptation and are more likely to sin.

1 Corinthians 1:2 NASB *"To the church of God which is in Corinth, to those who have been sanctified in Christ Jesus, saints by calling, with all who in every place call on the name of our Lord Jesus Christ, their Lord and ours."*

Also, remember that it's about running to God and repenting if you do sin. Don't hide like Adam and Eve did.

Proverbs 24:16 NIV *"for though the righteous fall seven times, they rise again, but the wicked stumble when calamity strikes."*

SAVED FROM WHAT?

So, what are we saved from? We are saved from the consequences of our sin. To be saved from the wages of sin (death) ultimately means to be saved from the wrath of God towards us if we were to die in our sin.

Our spirit will live somewhere forever, just as God Himself is eternal. We were created in God's image, and the part of us that is God-breathed is called our spirit. If we were to die in our sin, we would be eternally separated from God. This place of eternal separation is called Hell. I will not go into detail on Hell, but I will say that you don't want to go there and don't have to.

The good news is that we can be saved from eternal punishment and separation from God through faith and repentance. Regarding sin, it must be dealt with in order for God to be a just God. God is merciful, but He is also holy and just.

Romans 1:18 AMP *"For [God does not overlook sin and] the wrath of God is revealed from heaven against all ungodliness and unrighteousness of men who in their wickedness suppress and stifle the truth."*

Romans 5:8–9 NASB *"But God demonstrates His own love toward us, in that while we were still sinners, Christ died for us. [9] Much more then, having now been justified by His blood, we shall be saved from the wrath of God through Him."*

Hebrews 9:27–28 NASB *"And just as it is destined for people to die once, and after this comes judgment, [28] so Christ also,* *having been offered once to bear the sins of many, will appear a second time for salvation without reference to sin, to those who eagerly await Him."*

God created you with a free will. You have the power to accept or reject God's gift of salvation. Accepting God's gift requires repentance and submitting your will to God. You can't just ask for forgiveness without repenting and submitting to the Lordship of Jesus. You can no longer be your own god or serve the "god of this world" (Satan), as the Scripture says you cannot serve two masters.

2 Corinthians 4:4 AMP *"Among them the god of this world [Satan] has blinded the minds of the unbelieving to prevent them from seeing the illuminating light of the gospel of the glory of Christ, who is the image of God."*

The gospel (good news) of Jesus Christ is that the blood Jesus shed on the cross pays our debt in full if we accept it. Jesus dying in our place created a path back to God. Note that this is the only path back to God; there is no alternate path. I will go into more detail concerning Jesus being the only way in another section. Without God doing His part, we would be left in a fallen state, and there would be no opportunity for reconciliation. Left in this fallen state, we would be separated from God for all eternity.

Ephesians 2:1 AMP *"And you [He made alive when you] were [spiritually] dead and separated from Him because of your transgressions and sins."*

Eternal judgment or separation might sound extreme, yet nothing that is unholy can stand in His presence.

Psalm 5:4 NASB *"For You are not a God who takes pleasure in wickedness; No evil can dwell with You."*

Even if God didn't provide payment for our sin, He would still be just or justified if He condemned mankind. The good news is that God didn't leave us in our sin but provided a way for us to be saved. God demonstrated His love for us by paying our debt with the blood of His own Son, Jesus.

Romans 5:8 NIV *"But God demonstrates his own love for us in this: While we were still sinners, Christ died for us."*

Just as God has forgiven us, we need to forgive others (Matthew 6:12, 18:21–22). Know that forgiveness is not a feeling, but a release of a debt owed. When you forgive someone, you are releasing them from their obligation to you. When God forgave us, the debt for our sin was cancelled. This shows us that forgiveness acts like a legal transaction.

Forgiving someone who has hurt you also releases you. Not forgiving them is like taking poison and hoping the other person will die. Unforgiveness can also give the enemy a foothold in your life and cause you more harm than it's worth.

Matthew 6:15 NIV *"But if you do not forgive others their sins, your Father will not forgive your sins."*

JESUS – THE SON OF GOD – GOD THE SON

John 1:29 AMP *"The next day he saw Jesus coming to him and said, "Look! The Lamb of God who takes away the sin of the world!"*

Jesus taught with authority, unlike the religious leaders of the day (Matthew 7:29).
Jesus healed the sick (Matthew 4:23).
Opened blind eyes (Mark 10:46–52).
Opened deaf ears (Mark 7:31–37).
Raised Lazarus from the dead (John 11:38–44).
Walked on water (Matthew 14:25).
Stopped a storm with words (Matthew 8:23–27).
Jesus took a couple of fishes and loaves of bread and multiplied them, enough for thousands to eat on at least two occasions (John 6:10–13).
Jesus cast out demons from people (Matthew 8:28–32).

John 21:25 AMP *"And there are also many other things which Jesus did, which if they were recorded one by one, I suppose that even the world itself could not contain the books that would be written."*

John 10:38 AMP *"But if I am doing them, even if you do not believe Me or have faith in Me, [at least] believe the works [that I do—admit that they are the works of God], so that you may know and keep on knowing [clearly—without any doubt] that the Father is in Me, and I am in the Father [that is, I am One with Him]."*

God the Father raising Jesus from the dead validated that Jesus was the Son of God. We will cover many convincing proofs of the resurrection of Jesus in the section titled "Jesus crucified and resurrected."

Romans 6:9 AMP *"Because we know [the self-evident truth] that Christ, having been raised from the dead, will never die again; death no longer has power over Him."*

Matthew 28:6 NASB *"He is not here, for He has risen, just as He said. Come, see the place where He was lying."*

Acts 1:3 NASB *"To these He also presented Himself alive after His suffering, by many convincing proofs, appearing to them over a period of forty days and speaking of things regarding the kingdom of God."*

Not only did Jesus perform signs and wonders, but He empowered His disciples to do the same.

Luke 9:1-2 NASB *"Now He called the twelve together and gave them power and authority over all the demons, and the power to heal diseases.² And He sent them out to proclaim the kingdom of God and to perform healing."*

And it doesn't stop there. Jesus has given all believers the power to do what He did through the Holy Spirit.

John 14:12 AMP *"I assure you and most solemnly say to you, anyone who believes in Me [as Savior] will also do the things that I do; and he will do even greater things than these [in extent and outreach], because I am going to the Father."*

This empowerment given to believers to pray for the sick to be healed and cast out demons is unique to Christianity. Other religions might have some truth, compelling arguments, and even high moral standards, but there is only one true God who has the power to save, heal, and deliver.

Jesus is not only the Son of God, but He is also God the Son. This is a very important core belief of the Christian faith. This is where you will lose some who seem to believe what Scripture says concerning who Jesus is but really do not. Some other religions will say Jesus was a prophet, a holy man, or maybe a wise teacher. But if you believe what Jesus said along with the entirety of scripture, Jesus is God the Son as well as the Son of God.

What does it mean to say that Jesus is God the Son? God has chosen to reveal Himself as three distinct persons: God the Father, God the Son, and God the Holy Spirit. This is either referred to as the Trinity, the Triune God, or the Godhead. These terms are not in the Bible, but Bible teachers have used them to try and explain how God has chosen to reveal Himself to us. The Scriptures make it clear that, even with these distinctions, there is only one God.

We can establish the deity of Jesus through scripture. Jesus was God who came in the flesh to represent Himself within His creation, so that we could relate to Him as well as accomplish paying the debt owed for our sins.

Looking at John Chapter 1, you will find that Jesus is called the Word. The key is in verse 14, which says, "And the Word became flesh."

John 1:1,14 NASB *"In the beginning was the Word, and the Word was with God, and the Word was God."* [14] *"And the Word became flesh, and dwelt among us; and we saw His glory, glory as of the only Son from the Father, full of grace and truth."*

Let's take these verses; every time it says "Word," let's substitute it with Jesus.

1. In the beginning was **Jesus**, and **Jesus** was with God, and **Jesus** was God. 14. And **Jesus** became flesh and dwelt among us; and we saw His glory, glory as of the only Son from the Father, full of grace and truth.

Colossians 2:9 NASB *"For in Him all the fullness of Deity dwells in bodily form,"*

Colossians 1:15–17, 19 NIV *"The Son is the image of the invisible God, the firstborn over all creation.* [16] *For in him all things were created: things in heaven and on earth, visible and invisible, whether thrones or powers or rulers or authorities; all things have been created through him and for him.* [17] *He is before all things, and in him all things hold together...... * [19] *For God was pleased to have all his fullness dwell in him,"*

Jesus uses the term "I AM" seven times in the book of John. The term "I AM" is what God called Himself when Moses encountered God in the Old Testament.

Exodus 3:14 NIV *God said to Moses, "I am who I am. This is what you are to say to the Israelites: 'I am, has sent me to you."*

Jesus knew the scriptures and knew that the people listening to Him would know what He meant when He said, "I AM." If Jesus was just a prophet, He would not have used this terminology, knowing that those who heard Him would have considered it blasphemy.

John 6:35: I am the bread of life.
John 8:12: I am the light of the world.
John 10:9: I am the door.
John 10:11: I am the good shepherd.
John 11:25–26: I am the resurrection and the life.
John 14:6: I am the way, the truth, and the life.
John 15:5: I am the vine.

He also uses the term "I AM" when talking to the Pharisees.

John 8:58–59 NASB *"Jesus said to them, "Truly, truly I say to you, before Abraham was born, I am." ⁵⁹Therefore they picked up stones to throw at Him, but Jesus hid Himself and left the temple grounds."*

For Jesus to refer to Himself as "I AM" was the same as saying, I am God or equal with God. This was considered blasphemy by the Pharisees, and that is why they wanted to stone Him to death. The punishment for many sins in the old covenant was death.

Another thing that would have been forbidden was that Jesus accepted worship. No one who was just a prophet would have accepted worship. You see this with the apostles Barnabas and Paul; when some tried to worship them, they said, "No, we are just men," telling them to stop (Acts 14:15). If Jesus was just a man, He would have told them not to worship Him.

Matthew 14:33 NASB *"And those who were in the boat worshiped Him, saying, "You are truly God's Son."*

John 9:37–38 NASB *"Jesus said to him, "You have both seen Him, and He is the one who is talking with you." ³⁸And he said, "I believe, Lord." And he worshiped Him."*

John 20:28 NASB *"Thomas answered and said to Him, "My Lord and my God!"*

Matthew 28:16–17 AMP *"Now the eleven disciples went to Galilee, to the mountain which Jesus had designated. ¹⁷And when they saw Him, they worshiped Him; but some doubted [that it was really He]."*

Here are some other examples of people bowing before Jesus, and again, this would have been forbidden if Jesus was just a Rabbi. Matthew 15:25, Matthew 8:2, Matthew 20:20, and Matthew 9:18.

> But if you believe what Jesus said along with the entirety of Scripture, Jesus is God the Son as well as the Son of God.

JESUS IS THE ONLY WAY

Romans 3:23 NASB *"For all have sinned and fall short of the glory of God."*

What problem did this create? Can this problem be solved, and if so, how?

Romans 6:23 NASB *"For the wages of sin is death, but the gracious gift of God is eternal life in Christ Jesus our Lord."*

The problem is that sin has the consequence of death. From the day we were born, we had the death penalty against us. The verdict was guilty, and the penalty was death. Could we pay the debt to solve the problem for ourselves? No, God's requirement was a perfect sacrifice, so we are disqualified because of sin.

God knew that He would have to provide the payment on our behalf for our sins in order to reconcile us back to Himself. Jesus was the only man, born of a virgin, who lived a sinless life and was therefore qualified to be the sacrifice.

We can never earn our own salvation. We cannot reconcile ourselves to God through our own efforts. Just as the first man, Adam, sinned, causing the fall of man (Romans 5:12), the last man Christ Jesus died to redeem man (Romans 5:15).

Plainly put, Jesus died in our place. Jesus died as a substitute in our place, and His substitution would cover the debt for all who would believe.

Hebrews 9:22 NLT *"In fact, according to the law of Moses, nearly everything was purified with blood. For without the shedding of blood, there is no forgiveness."*

Hebrews 10:10 NASB *"By this will, we have been sanctified through the offering of the body of Jesus Christ once for all time."*

John 14:6 NASB *"Jesus said to him, 'I am the way, and the truth, and the life; no one comes to the Father except through Me.'"*

Acts 4:12 NASB *"And there is salvation in no one else; for there is no other name under heaven that has been given among mankind by which we must be saved."*

Concerning our own fallen state, **Psalm 51:5 NLT** says, *"For I was born a sinner - yes, from the moment my mother conceived me."*

Concerning Jesus's qualifications, it's important to know that Jesus had no earthly father but was conceived by the Holy Spirit. Therefore, Jesus was not born into sin.

Luke 1:26–31 NLT *"In the sixth month of Elizabeth's pregnancy, God sent the angel Gabriel to Nazareth, a village in Galilee,[27] to a virgin named Mary. She was engaged to be married to a man named Joseph, a descendant of King David.[28] Gabriel appeared to her and said, "Greetings, favored woman! The Lord is with you!"[29] Confused and disturbed, Mary tried to think what the angel could mean.[30] "Don't be afraid, Mary," the angel told her, "For you have found favor with God![31] You will conceive and give birth to a son, and you will name him Jesus."*

Then, after Jesus was born, He lived a sinless life.

1 Peter 2:22 NIV *"He committed no sin, and no deceit was found in his mouth."*

2 Corinthians 5:21 NASB *"He made Him who knew no sin to be sin in our behalf, so that we might become the righteousness of God in Him."*

Being conceived by the Holy Spirit and then living a sinless life sets up the qualification for Jesus to die on behalf of all mankind. Unlike the sacrifices that were made in the Old Testament of animals that only temporarily covered the sins of God's children, the blood of Jesus would pay in full the price for the sin of all mankind.

Romans 3:25 NIV *"God presented Christ as a sacrifice of atonement, through the shedding of his blood—to be received by faith. He did this to demonstrate his righteousness, because in his forbearance he had left the sins committed beforehand unpunished."*

Hebrews 9:12 NASB *"And not through the blood of goats and calves, but through His own blood, He entered the holy place once for all time, having obtained eternal redemption."*

Colossians 2:14 NIV *"Having canceled the charge of our legal indebtedness, which stood against us and condemned us; he has taken it away, nailing it to the cross.*

1 John 5:12–13 AMP *"He who has the Son [by accepting Him as Lord and Savior] has the life [that is eternal]; he who does not have the Son of God [by personal faith] does not have the life."*

What Jesus did on the cross created the opportunity for us to repent, confess, believe, surrender, and be saved. God's act of love saves us and restores our relationship with Him once we accept it.

As we have established, there is only one true God and only one path back into a right relationship with Him. I love how John, inspired by the Holy Spirit, included the message to all believers that you can know that you are saved. This assurance is not just words on a page; God confirms it in our hearts and minds through the work of the Holy Spirit.

1 John 5:13 NASB *"These things I have written to you who believe in the name of the Son of God, so that you may know that you have eternal life."*

Jesus was the only man, born of a virgin, who lived a sinless life and was therefore qualified to be the sacrifice. We can never earn our own salvation. We cannot reconcile ourselves to God through our own efforts.

IN THE BEGINNING

Let's back up and examine the creation story as recorded in the Old Testament. To set the stage, God is in heaven (outside of time and space), and the physical world as we know it does not yet exist. God created everything we can and can't see over a six-day period, and on the seventh day, it says He rested.

Colossians 1:16 NASB *"For by Him all things were created, both in the heavens and on earth, visible and invisible, whether thrones, or dominions, or rulers, or authorities—all things have been created through Him and for Him."*

Here is the creation story as described in Genesis.

Genesis 1:1–5 NIV *"In the beginning God created the heavens and the earth. ²Now the earth was formless and empty, darkness was over the surface of the deep, and the Spirit of God was hovering over the waters. ³And God said, "Let there be light," and there was light. ⁴God saw that the light was good, and he separated the light from the darkness. ⁵God called the light "day," and the darkness he called "night." And there was evening, and there was morning—the first day."*

The story goes on to describe God creating all living things, and then finally on day six, God creates man. The one thing that is special about man is that God created man in His own image.

Genesis 1:26–28 AMP *"Then God said, "Let Us (Father, Son, Holy Spirit) make man in Our image, according to Our likeness [not physical, but a spiritual personality and moral likeness]; and let them have complete authority over the fish of the sea, the birds of the air, the cattle, and over the entire earth, and over everything that creeps and crawls on the earth."* [27] *So God created man in His own image, in the image and likeness of God He created him; male and female He created them."*

God gave Adam and Eve specific instructions to refrain from just one thing.

Genesis 2:17 AMP *"But [only] from the tree of the knowledge (recognition) of good and evil you shall not eat, otherwise on the day that you eat from it, you shall most certainly die [because of your disobedience]."*

At some point, Adam and Eve were tempted by Satan who had taken on the form of a serpent. The result of that temptation was disobedience. This act of disobedience is typically called the fall of man and caused a separation in relationship between man and God.

Adam and Eve had dominion over all living things and had every resource they needed. The Garden of Eden was a beautiful place. It's hard to understand why they listened to Satan and not God. Everything was peaceful before they disobeyed God, but now things were about to drastically change. Creation itself, including man, would now be subject to a curse that ushered in death.

1 Samuel 15:23 KJV *"For rebellion is as the sin of witchcraft, and stubbornness is as iniquity and idolatry. Because thou hast* *rejected the word of the Lord, he hath also rejected thee from being king."*

Isaiah 59:2 NASB *"But your wrongdoings have caused a separation between you and your God, and your sins have hidden His face from you so that He does not hear."*

Romans 6:23 NLT *"For the wages of sin is death, but the free gift of God is eternal life through Christ Jesus our Lord."*

The act of disobedience by Adam and Eve is what caused the need for redemption in the first place. Now, man has a problem that he can't fix. God, in His grace and mercy, sets into motion the solution to the problem Adam and Eve created.

> The one thing that is special about man is that God created man in His image.

A BROKEN RELATIONSHIP

As humans, we try to categorize sin and even create our own moral standard. There is even a current trend to redefine what is good and call it evil and embrace that which is evil and call it good. The problem with us creating our own moral standard is that God is the only one who is holy and has the authority to establish what is good and what is evil.

It's worth reiterating what problem was created by Adam and Eve's sin.

Psalm 5:4 AMP *"For You are not a God who takes pleasure in wickedness; No evil [person] dwells with You."*

For this reason, Adam and Eve were kicked out of the Garden of Eden so that they would not also eat from the Tree of Life. God chose to fix the problem man created before it became permanent so that man would not be trapped in this fallen state forever.

Genesis 3:22–24 NASB *"Then the Lord God said, "Behold, the man has become like one of Us, knowing good and evil; and now, he might reach out with his hand, and take fruit also from the tree of life, and eat, and live forever" 23 therefore the Lord God sent him out of the Garden of Eden, to cultivate the ground from which he was taken. 24 So He drove the man out; and at the east of the Garden of Eden He stationed the cherubim and the flaming sword which turned every direction to guard the way to the tree of life."*

The Bible says that God visited Adam and Eve in the garden after they sinned.

Genesis 3:8 NLT *"When the cool evening breezes were blowing, the man and his wife heard the Lord God walking about in the garden. So, they hid from the Lord God among the trees."*

This wasn't the first time God interacted with Adam.

Genesis 2:19 NLT It says, *"So the Lord God formed from the ground all the wild animals and all the birds of the sky. He brought them to the man to see what he would call them, and the man chose a name for each one."*

The interactions God had with Adam tell us that God had a relationship with him, and they communicated. Their relationship was broken because of sin. But God was ahead of Adam and already had a plan in place.

1 Peter 1:19–20 TPT *"But the precious blood of Christ, who like a spotless, unblemished lamb was sacrificed for us. This was part of God's plan, for he was chosen and destined for this before the foundation of the earth was laid, but he has been made manifest in these last days for you."*

Sin disqualifies us from being in God's presence and separates us from Him. God did not want to leave man in this fallen state but provided an opportunity for man to be reconciled back to Himself. The death and resurrection of Jesus would provide this opportunity of reconciliation.

Romans 5:15–17 NASB *"But the gracious gift is not like the offense. For if by the offense of the one the many died, much more did the grace of God and the gift by the grace of the one Man, Jesus Christ, overflow to the many.[16]The gift is not like that which came through the one who sinned; for on the one hand the judgment arose from one offense, resulting in condemnation, but on the other hand the gracious gift arose from many offenses, resulting in justification. [17]For if by the offense of the one, death reigned through the one, much more will those who receive the abundance of grace and of the gift of righteousness reign in life through the One, Jesus Christ."*

The ultimate tragedy of the story was a broken relationship between God and his creation. Victory was achieved through Jesus' death and resurrection which provides the opportunity for reconciliation with God.

THE BIGGER PICTURE

God is not bound by time in the same way we are. God is omniscient (all-knowing), omnipotent (all-powerful), and sovereign (has ultimate control of the bigger picture). God saw His creation fail before it actually played out and chose to provide a way for us to be reconciled to Him.

1 Peter 1:18–20 NASB *"Knowing that you were not redeemed with perishable things like silver or gold from your futile way of life inherited from your forefathers,[19]but with precious blood, as of a lamb unblemished and spotless, the blood of Christ.[20]For He was foreknown before the foundation of the world, but has appeared in these last times for the sake of you."*

We can see the plan God established in the Old Testament unfold in the New Testament.

Micah 5:2 NASB *"But as for you, Bethlehem Ephrathah, too little to be among the clans of Judah, from you one will come forth for Me to be ruler in Israel. His times of coming forth are from long ago, from the days of eternity."*

Isaiah 7:14 AMP *"Therefore the Lord Himself will give you a sign: Listen carefully, the virgin will conceive and give birth to a son, and she will call his name Immanuel (God with us)."*

There are over 100 prophecies in the Old Testament that are fulfilled in the New Testament by Jesus. I read one article by the Fellowship of Israel Related Ministries that said, "Jesus, Yeshua in Hebrew, fulfilled not just the 48 specifically Messianic prophecies. In fact, He fulfilled more than 324 individual prophecies that related to the Messiah." But for argument's sake, what if He only fulfilled eight prophecies? The odds of just eight prophecies being fulfilled by one person would be 1 in 10^{17} (1 in 100,000,000,000,000,000).

The fulfillment of all these prophecies, from the Old Testament to the New Testament, is one of the unique components of our Christian faith. Evidence upon evidence brings us assurance that Jesus is the Messiah. In Isaiah chapter 53 alone, Jesus fulfills 7 major Messianic prophecies.

Then, a point of authenticity of the New Testament was that actual eyewitnesses wrote it during their lifetimes. Mark and Luke might be the only exceptions, but the documentation is paralleled in Matthew and John, who were with Jesus during His earthly ministry. Mark traveled with the Apostle Peter and Apostle Paul at different times, and Luke traveled with Paul.

This big picture comes down to a love story between God and His creation. A story of love, compassion, mercy, grace, and redemption played out on a stage called Earth.

John 3:16 NASB *"For God so loved the world, that He gave His only Son, so that everyone who believes in Him will not perish but have eternal life."*

Everything God does is intentional and has a purpose.

Ephesians 1:11 NASB *"In Him we also have obtained an inheritance, having been predestined according to the purpose of Him who works all things in accordance with the plan of His will."*

Isaiah 46:10–11 NASB *"Declaring the end from the beginning, And from ancient times things which have not been done, saying, 'My plan will be established, and I will accomplish all My good pleasure [11] Calling a bird of prey from the east, the man of My purpose from a distant country. Truly I have spoken; truly I will bring it to pass. I have planned it, I will certainly do it."*

And thankfully, God still moves and speaks to us today. We can experience the presence of God for ourselves. We are not left with just words on a page; God lives in us and works through us.

John 16:13 AMP *"But when He, the Spirit of Truth, comes, He will guide you into all the truth [full and complete truth]. For He will not speak on His own initiative, but He will speak whatever He hears [from the Father—the message regarding the Son], and He will disclose to you what is to come [in the future]."*

> God can see the end from the beginning and can help us navigate our lives if we are submitted to Him and go to Him for direction.

JESUS CRUCIFIED AND RESURRECTED

It seems improbable that if Jesus was performing countless miracles, somehow, He would end up being sentenced to death—death on a cross of all things. This is where the pride of the religious leaders came in. The religious leaders of the day became jealous of Jesus and the attention He was getting. The very Messiah they said they were looking for—they didn't recognize Him as the Messiah but saw Him as a threat to their position. If they had understood the Scriptures they said they followed, they would have seen that the Messiah was to come as a baby, not a full-grown man. They would have known He wasn't coming to restore Israel and the throne of David on His first visit, but He was to come as the sacrificial lamb to take away the sin of the world (John 1:29).

The religious leaders were so focused on the Ten Commandments—in reality, all 613 Jewish commandments (mitzvot in Hebrew) extracted from the Old Testament—that they missed loving and serving God.

One of the things that really seemed to upset the religious leaders was when Jesus would heal someone on the Sabbath. You would think that they would be amazed that He had the ability to heal people. Who else among them was healing people or casting out demons? I find it amazing that instead of celebrating all the signs and wonders, they wanted to criticize what day He was doing it on.

Matthew 12:8 NLT *"For the Son of Man is Lord, even over the Sabbath!"*

What this means is that He cannot break something He created and is Lord over. He also gave them an example to try and help them understand that they were missing the point.

Luke 14:5 NASB *"And He said to them, "Which one of you will have a son or an ox fall into a well, and will not immediately pull him out on a Sabbath day?"*

Had the religious leaders realized who Jesus really was, it's highly unlikely they would have had Him arrested by the Romans and demanded that He be crucified. They were blinded because of their pride. However, God orchestrated all of the events surrounding Jesus' death so that they would fulfill the Old Testament prophecies. As horrible as it may seem that Jesus died this gruesome death, it had to happen this way to fulfill prophecy and create the path back to God.

John 12:40 NLT *"The Lord has blinded their eyes and hardened their hearts so that their eyes cannot see, and their hearts cannot understand, and they cannot turn to me and have me heal them."*

Without these events playing out, our ability to be forgiven for our sins would not even exist. God was most assuredly involved in how these events played out.

John 12:32–33 AMP *"And I, if and when I am lifted up from the earth [on the cross], will draw all people to Myself [Gentiles, as well as Jews]." ³³He said this to indicate the kind of death by which He was to die."*

Jesus was not actually crucified by the Jews but by the Romans. The Jewish religious leaders demanded that the Roman authorities crucify Jesus. They accused Jesus of saying He was a king, saying it violated Roman law and was punishable by death (Matthew 27:11–12). The story of Jesus' death, burial, and resurrection is recorded in John Chapters 19–21 and is worth reading the entire account.

Many prophecies in the Old Testament were fulfilled on the day of Jesus' crucifixion, even down to what would happen to His clothes. This only confirms that God set this all up and saw it happen well before it actually happened. Even Jesus told everyone what was going to happen ahead of time.

John 2:19 NASB *"Jesus answered them, "Destroy this temple, and in three days I will raise it up."*

The overwhelming evidence of the resurrection of our Lord and Savior is foundational. Christianity hinges on the resurrection of Jesus. Even in Romans 10:9, the language Paul used was "and believe God raised Him from the dead, and you will be saved" as part of our faith declaration.

How can anyone be so sure Jesus did resurrect from the dead, you might ask? Evidence is used in a court of law to establish what has already happened. So, what do we know? Were we actually there to witness any of this ourselves? Like in a court of law, those examining a case don't have to have been there to know what happened. As long as there is sufficient evidence, a verdict can be established. We can start with what Scripture says about the events right after the crucifixion.

Matthew 27:54 NASB *"Now as for the centurion and those who were with him keeping guard over Jesus, when they saw the earthquake and the other things that were happening, they became extremely frightened and said, "Truly this was the Son of God!"*

Then, Jesus was put in a borrowed tomb. The religious leaders were so concerned that Jesus' followers were going to steal the body that they asked the Romans to guard the tomb.

Matthew 27:62–66 NASB *"Now on the next day, that is, the day which is after the preparation, the chief priests and the Pharisees gathered together with Pilate,⁶³ and they said, "Sir, we remember that when that deceiver was still alive, He said, 'After three days I am rising.⁶⁴Therefore, give orders for the tomb to be made secure until the third day; otherwise, His disciples may come and steal Him and say to the people, 'He has risen from the dead,' and the last deception will be worse than the first." ⁶⁵Pilate said to them, "You have a guard; go, make it as secure as you know how." ⁶⁶ And they went and made the tomb secure with the guard, sealing the stone."*

The tomb was sealed, and the consequence of that seal being broken would have been significant, so the soldiers assigned to the tomb were not going to let someone come and steal the body. But when God sends an angel, well...

Matthew 28:1–7 NASB *"Now after the Sabbath, as it began to dawn toward the first day of the week, Mary Magdalene and the other Mary came to look at the tomb.² And behold, a severe earthquake had occurred, for an angel of the Lord descended from heaven and came and rolled away the stone and sat upon it. ³ And his appearance was like lightning, and his clothing as white as snow. ⁴ The guards shook from fear of him and became like dead men. ⁵ And the angel said to the women, "[Do not be afraid; for I know that you are looking for Jesus who has been crucified. ⁶ He is not here, for He has risen, just as He said. Come, see the place where He was lying. ⁷ And go quickly and tell His disciples that He has risen from the dead; and behold, He is going ahead of you to Galilee. There you will see Him; behold, I have told you."*

Then, in verses **16–20**, *"But the eleven disciples proceeded to Galilee, to the mountain which Jesus had designated to them.¹⁷ And when they saw Him, they worshiped Him; but some were doubtful. ¹⁸ And Jesus came up and spoke to them, saying, "All authority in heaven and on earth has been given to Me.¹⁹ Go, therefore, and make disciples of all the nations, baptizing them in the name of the Father and the Son and the Holy Spirit,²⁰ teaching them to follow all that I commanded you; and behold, I am with you always, to the end of the age."*

In 1 Corinthians 15:6, Paul said that Jesus appeared to the 12 disciples and then to over 500 people at one time after the resurrection. The book of Acts says that Jesus was among them and appeared to the disciples over 40 days, continuing to teach them before He ascended into heaven.

Acts 1:1–3 NASB *"The first account I composed, Theophilus, about all that Jesus began to do and teach, ²until the day when He was taken up to heaven, after He had given orders by the Holy Spirit to the apostles whom He had chosen.³To these He also presented Himself alive after His suffering, by many convincing proofs, appearing to them over a period of forty days and speaking of things regarding the kingdom of God."*

Then, there is what comes next in the lives of Jesus's followers. Jesus instructs His disciples to wait for the promised Holy Spirit. Through the Holy Spirit, the ministry of Jesus would not only continue, but it would grow exponentially. Jesus sent the Holy Spirit, who then empowered His followers to do exactly what He did. Heal the sick, cast out demons, and even raise the dead.

A book called "Miracles Today" by Craig S. Keener says, "In 2006, a Pew Forum survey of just ten countries on four continents suggested that about two hundred million Pentecostal and Protestant charismatics in those countries alone claim to have witnessed divine healing. Perhaps more surprisingly, some 39 percent of Christians in those countries who are not Pentecostals or Protestant charismatics also claim to have witnessed divine healing. Hundreds of millions of people around the world claim to have witnessed such experiences." This is mind-boggling evidence that God is still involved in believers' lives today and is showing Himself to be faithful to the promises that He made.

Then what about the apostles, and why did they continue to follow Jesus if He was just dead? Why were they still willing to die and eventually be martyred for their faith? If Jesus had just died and not shown Himself to His followers and not sent the Holy Spirit with the power to heal and deliver, the whole thing would have unraveled, and you would not be reading this book right now. Jesus is alive, and as many as believe in Him are given the right to be called the children of God.

John 1:12–13 NASB *"But as many as received Him, to them He gave the right to become children of God, to those who believe in His name,¹³ who were born, not of blood, nor of the will of the flesh, nor of the will of a man, but of God."*

> The overwhelming evidence of the resurrection of our Lord and Savior is foundational.

SALVATION IS A PROCESS

I have heard it preached that you are saved, you're being saved, and you will be saved. This really lays out that we don't just say a prayer, continue living the same way and someday end up in heaven. There needs to be a true-life transformation.

2 Corinthians 13:5 NASB *"Test yourselves to see if you are in the faith; examine yourselves! Or do you not recognize this about yourselves, that Jesus Christ is in you unless indeed you fail the test?"*

For Jesus to be your Lord means that you submit your will to God and live the way God says to live. Don't worry; God is there to help you every step of the way. At the beginning of your walk with God, you repented, confessed, believed, surrendered, and were saved.

John 1:12 NLT *"But to all who believed him and accepted him, he gave the right to become children of God."*

You believed in your heart concerning Jesus's death and resurrection and confessed Jesus as Lord.

Romans 10:9–10 NLT *"If you openly declare that Jesus is Lord and believe in your heart that God raised him from the dead, you will be saved.[10]For it is by believing in your heart that you are made right with God, and it is by openly declaring your faith that you are saved."*

Your spirit, which is eternal, was saved and made new. You were declared righteous, which means you are in right standing with God.

2 Corinthians 5:21 NASB *"He made Him who knew no sin to be sin in our behalf, so that we might become the righteousness of God in Him."*

Then comes living out your faith in your daily life, but there is a challenge. You are made up of your soul (mind, will, and emotions), your spirit (that which is eternal or God-breathed), and your body (your flesh). Your soul, spirit, and flesh are going to be at odds with each other. Your body desires the things of the flesh, and your spirit desires the things of God. Your mind is in the middle, where a battle for control takes place.

Romans 12:2 NLT "Don't *copy the behavior and customs of this world, but let God transform you into a new person by changing the way you think. Then you will learn to know God's will for you, which is good and pleasing and perfect."*

You must die to yourself and submit your will to God daily.

Luke 9:23 AMP *"And He was saying to them all, "If anyone wishes to follow Me [as My disciple], he must deny himself [set aside selfish interests] and take up his cross daily [expressing a willingness to endure whatever may come] and follow Me [believing in Me, conforming to My example in living and, if need be, suffering or perhaps dying because of faith in Me]."*

Denying yourself daily is part of the process of being saved. And someday, if your physical body dies or Jesus comes back first, your spirit will go to be with God. Through physical death or Jesus' return, believers will finally reach the finish line of salvation.

2 Corinthians 5:8 NLT *"Yes, we are fully confident, and we would rather be away from these earthly bodies, for then we will be at home with the Lord."*

1 Corinthians 15:50–52 NASB *"Now I say this, brothers and sisters, that flesh and blood cannot inherit the kingdom of God; nor does the perishable inherit the imperishable.[51]Behold, I am telling you a mystery; we will not all sleep, but we will all be changed,[52]in a moment, in the twinkling of an eye, at the last trumpet; for the trumpet will sound, and the dead will be raised imperishable, and we will be changed."*

The promise is eternal life for those who believe.

John 3:16 NASB *"For God so loved the world, that He gave His only Son, so that everyone who believes in Him will not perish but have eternal life."*

Romans 6:23 NASB *"For the wages of sin is death, but the gracious gift of God is eternal life in Christ Jesus our Lord."*

1 John 5:11–12 NIV *"And this is the testimony: God has given us eternal life, and this life is in his Son.[12]Whoever has the Son has life; whoever does not have the Son of God does not have life."*

Part of the journey is learning to trust God for everything, not just eternal salvation. You would think if we could trust God concerning eternity, it would be easy to trust God for temporal things. From my own experience, connecting the dots on this principle can be difficult.

Matthew 6:31–34 NIV *"So do not worry, saying, 'What shall we eat?' or 'What shall we drink?' or 'What shall we wear?' [32] For the pagans run after all these things, and your heavenly Father knows that you need them. [33] But seek first his kingdom and his righteousness, and all these things will be given to you as well. [34] Therefore do not worry about tomorrow, for tomorrow will worry about itself. Each day has enough trouble of its own."*

God knows what we need and when we need it. Thankfully, God is faithful and is working behind the scenes on our behalf. God is orchestrating things concerning our lives here on earth and we can trust Him.

Leading up to this next verse, Paul talks about a believer who is submitted to the Lordship of Jesus.

Romans 8:28 NASB *"And we know that God causes all things to work together for good to those who love God, to those who are called according to His purpose."*

There is a dying to yourself and submitting your will to God on a daily basis.

JESUS IS COMING BACK

Jesus came for the first time to fulfill Scripture concerning the role of the Messiah as the sacrificial lamb of God. Jesus said He was going back to the Father but that He would return. This is referred to as the second coming of Jesus. Let's look at some Scriptures concerning the second coming of Jesus.

John 14:3–4 NLT *"When everything is ready, I will come and get you, so that you will always be with me where I am.⁴And you know the way to where I am going."*

The first time Jesus came, He was to be crucified and resurrected. The second coming of Jesus will be as the King of kings and the Lord of lords.

Revelation 19:11–16 NLT *"Then I saw heaven opened, and a white horse was standing there. Its rider was named Faithful and True, for he judges fairly and wages a righteous war.¹²His eyes were like flames of fire, and on his head were many crowns. A name was written on him that no one understood except himself.¹³He wore a robe dipped in blood, and his title was the Word of God.¹⁴The armies of heaven, dressed in the finest of pure white linen, followed him on white horses.¹⁵From his mouth came a sharp sword to strike down the nations. He will rule them with an iron rod. He will release the fierce wrath of God, the Almighty, like juice flowing from a winepress.¹⁶On his robe at his thigh was written this title: King of all kings and Lord of all lords."*

No one knows the day or hour of the second coming of Jesus but God the Father, but the overwhelming instructions given in Scripture can be summed up by saying, "Get ready, be ready, stay ready."

Matthew 24:42,44 NASB *"Therefore be on the alert, for you do not know which day your Lord is coming. [44] For this reason you must be ready as well; for the Son of Man is coming at an hour when you do not think He will."*

When Jesus comes back, He will judge the living and the dead.

John 5:26–27 NLT *"The Father has life in himself, and he has granted that same life-giving power to his Son. [27] And he has given him authority to judge everyone because he is the Son of Man.*

The talk of judgment might sound alarming. For the believer, the second coming of Jesus is something to anticipate—not fear. Remember, Jesus is our savior and has saved us from the wrath of God against those who never repent—those who never accepted the gift of salvation.

Titus 2:13 NASB *"looking for the blessed hope and the appearing of the glory of our great God and Savior, Christ Jesus."*

Hebrews 9:28 NASB *"So Christ also, having been offered once to bear the sins of many, will appear a second time for salvation without reference to sin, to those who eagerly await Him."*

REVIEW

God created man in His image and gave man dominion over Earth (Genesis 1:26–28).

Man sinned and was separated from God (Genesis 3:6, 22–24).

God came in the flesh as Jesus Christ (1 John 4:2).

Jesus was born of a virgin (Luke 1:26-33).

Jesus lived a sinless life (1 Peter 2:22).

Jesus was crucified on a cross, and His body was put in a borrowed tomb (1 Corinthians 15:4).

Jesus was resurrected from the dead by God the Father (Romans 10:9).

Jesus is now seated at the right hand of God the Father in heaven (Hebrews 1:3).

Everyone has sinned and falls short of God's moral standard (Romans 3:23).

Faith in the life, death, and resurrection of Jesus Christ, repentance, and declaring Jesus as Lord results in salvation for those who believe.

Romans 10:9–10, John 1:12-13, John 3:16, John 5:24, John 3:14–21, John 3:34–36, 1 John 4:15, 1 Peter 1:20–23, Romans 5:17, Acts 2:21, Acts 10:43, Acts 16:31, Acts 2:38, Ephesians 1:13–14, Ephesians 2:8–9, 1 Timothy 1:15, John 6:39–40, Romans 1:16, Romans 5:1

Jesus will return as King of kings and Lord of lords (Revelation 19:11–16).

Jesus has been given all authority under heaven and earth by God the Father (John 5:26–29).

One day, at the end of the age, Jesus will judge the living and the dead (John 5:26–29).

HEAVEN AND ANGELS

Heaven, where God the Father and God the Son are now, existed before our physical world existed. God is not bound by time but has existed outside of time and space as we know it. God has no beginning and no end and was not created (1 Timothy 6:15–16, Revelation 1:8 and 4:8, Psalm 90:2).

When the Bible refers to heaven or the heavens, it is referring to either the earth's atmosphere, space outside of the earth's atmosphere, or where God the Father and Jesus are now. The heaven we are going to talk about is the latter.

The Bible says that God the Father, is in heaven. In the Lord's prayer, Jesus taught His disciples to pray, "Our Father, who art in heaven." Later Jesus said He had to go back to be with the Father before He could send the Holy Spirit.

John 16:5–6 NASB *"But now I am going to Him who sent Me; and none of you asks Me, 'Where are You going?' ⁶But because I have said these things to you, grief has filled your heart."*

John 14:2–3 NASB *"In My Father's house are many rooms; if that were not so, I would have told you, because I am going there to prepare a place for you.³ And if I go and prepare a place for you, I am coming again and will take you to Myself, so that where I am, there you also will be."*

When our physical bodies die, it's not the end; it's just a new beginning.

2 Corinthians 5:6–8 NIV *"Therefore we are always confident and know that as long as we are at home in the body we are away from the Lord.⁷For we live by faith, not by sight.⁸We are confident, I say, and would prefer to be away from the body and at home with the Lord."*

Philippians 3:20–21 NIV *"But our citizenship is in heaven. And we eagerly await a Savior from there, the Lord Jesus Christ,²¹ who, by the power that enables him to bring everything under his control, will transform our lowly bodies so that they will be like his glorious body."*

Something that really stood out to me in this next passage in Revelation was that in eternity, after it's all said and done, we will not need the sun for light, but God is the light—just as it was on day one of creation.

Revelation 21:1–5, 22–23 NASB *"Then I saw a new heaven and a new earth; for the first heaven and the first earth passed away, and there is no longer any sea.²And I saw the holy city, new Jerusalem, coming down out of heaven from God, prepared as a bride adorned for her husband.³And I heard a loud voice from the throne, saying, "Behold, the tabernacle of God is among the people, and He will dwell among them, and they shall be His people, and God Himself will be among them,⁴and He will wipe away every tear from their eyes; and there will no longer be any death; there will no longer be any mourning, or crying, or pain; the first things have passed away."⁵And He who sits on the throne said, "Behold, I am making all things new." And He said, "Write, for these words are* *faithful and true."...... ^{22} I did not see a temple in the city, because the Lord God Almighty and the Lamb are its temple. ^{23} The city does not need the sun or the moon to shine on it, for the glory of God gives it light, and the Lamb is its lamp."*

The Bible also talks about angels and their role in helping believers.

Hebrews 1:14 NASB *"Are they not all ministering spirits, sent out to provide service for the sake of those who will inherit salvation?"*

Matthew 18:10 NASB *"See that you do not look down on one of these little ones; for I say to you that their angels in heaven continually see the face of My Father who is in heaven."*

Psalm 34:7 NASB *"The angel of the Lord encamps around those who fear Him and rescues them."*

Scripture also says this about angels.

Hebrews 13:2 NIV *"Do not forget to show hospitality to strangers, for by so doing some people have shown hospitality to angels without knowing it."*

Angels worship God, help those who are being saved; they are messengers and warriors. The angels that disobeyed God, along with Lucifer (Satan), were cast out of heaven and will one day face eternal judgment (2 Peter 2:4, Revelation 12:4, Jude 1:6).

BUT WAIT! THERE'S MORE

You might ask yourself, "Is there anything more?" The answer to this question is yes. There are three foundational components to our walk with God and some other things worth mentioning.

1) Putting your faith and trust in Jesus for salvation

2) Being baptized in water

3) Being Spirit-filled or being baptized in the Holy Spirit.

We have talked extensively about number 1: putting your faith in Jesus. In the sections to come, we will look closer at components 2 and 3.

Some other things Jesus taught us to do are to remember His sacrifice by taking communion, the great commission (being a witness of Jesus), prayer, fasting, giving, and serving. A significant amount of Jesus' teachings are about love and forgiveness. If you love God with all your heart, love yourself and others, and forgive yourself and others, you will live the life of a true believer.

WATER BAPTISM

The Bible says, "Believe and be baptized." The practice of the early church was to baptize new believers at conversion. Don't wait for a special sign or feeling. Baptism is a command and should be done out of obedience (Acts 2:38; Matthew 28:19). Water baptism is a physical act representing what you have already done in faith. Going under the water represents the death of your old self and coming out of the water represents coming alive in Christ or resurrecting with Christ. Water baptism is a public confession of believing in Jesus' redemptive work and declaring Him as your Lord and Savior.

Our faith needs to be public, not private.

Matthew 10:32–33 NLT *"Everyone who acknowledges me publicly here on earth, I will also acknowledge before my Father in heaven.³³But everyone who denies me here on earth, I will also deny before my Father in heaven."*

Jesus was baptized, so you should also be baptized. Jesus, the one who was without sin, didn't need to be baptized as a sign of repentance, but He always led by example. Something that might be controversial but needs to be stated; babies can't repent, believe, or confess anything. Therefore, you can dedicate babies, but to say you are baptizing them is not scriptural.

Mark 16:16 NASB *"The one who has believed and has been baptized will be saved; but the one who has not believed will be condemned."*

1 Peter 3:21 NASB *"Corresponding to that, baptism now saves you, not the removal of dirt from the flesh, but an appeal to God for a good conscience, through the resurrection of Jesus Christ."*

Matthew 28:19 AMP *"Go therefore and make disciples of all the nations [help the people to learn of Me, believe in Me, and obey My words], baptizing them in the name of the Father and of the Son and of the Holy Spirit."*

Peter 3:21 AMP *"Corresponding to that [rescue through the flood], baptism [which is an expression of a believer's new life in Christ] now saves you, not by removing dirt from the body, but by an appeal to God for a good (clear) conscience, [demonstrating what you believe to be yours] through the resurrection of Jesus Christ."*

Acts 2:38 NASB *"Peter said to them, "Repent, and each of you be baptized in the name of Jesus Christ for the forgiveness of your sins; and you will receive the gift of the Holy Spirit."*

Acts 2:41 AMP *"So then, those who accepted his message were baptized; and on that day about 3,000 souls were added [to the body of believers]."*

BAPTISM IN THE HOLY SPIRIT

The Apostles and early followers of Jesus were told to go and wait for the promised Holy Spirit. The Greek word translated to baptize in Acts 1:5 is *baptízō*. According to Strong's concordance for usage, "I dip, submerge, but specifically of ceremonial dipping; I baptize." Under the word study, it says, "*baptízō*, properly, 'submerge' (Souter); hence, baptize, to immerse (literally, 'dip under') implies submersion ('immersion')." Reading Acts 1:5 and Luke 24:49, with this definition in mind, Jesus is saying you will be baptized or submerged with the power and presence of the Holy Spirit.

Luke 24:49 AMP *"Listen carefully: I am sending the Promise of My Father [the Holy Spirit] upon you; but you are to remain in the city [of Jerusalem] until you are clothed (fully equipped) with power from on high."*

Acts 1:4-5 NIV *"On one occasion, while he was eating with them, he gave them this command: "Do not leave Jerusalem, but wait for the gift my Father promised, which you have heard me speak about. 'For John baptized with water, but in a few days you will be baptized with the Holy Spirit."*

They walked with Jesus; they were His chosen ones; they already believed in Jesus, repented, and confessed Jesus as Lord, so what was missing? Jesus Himself didn't start His earthly ministry until He was baptized in the Holy Spirit. The first miracle of Jesus, turning water into wine (John 2:11), was after being baptized in water and by the Holy Spirit. Just like water baptism, if Jesus, the Son of God, needed to be baptized or filled with the Holy Spirit, so do we.

Matthew 3:16–17 NIV *"As soon as Jesus was baptized, he went up out of the water. At that moment heaven was opened, and he saw the Spirit of God descending like a dove and alighting on him.[17] And a voice from heaven said, "This is my Son, whom I love; with him I am well pleased."*

Acts 10:38 NASB *"You know of Jesus of Nazareth, how God anointed Him with the Holy Spirit and with power, and how He went about doing good and healing all who were oppressed by the devil, for God was with Him."*

Concerning us:

Acts 1:8 AMP *"But you will receive power and ability when the Holy Spirit comes upon you; and you will be My witnesses [to tell people about Me] both in Jerusalem and in all Judea, and Samaria, and even to the ends of the earth."*

Acts 2:38 NLT *"Peter replied, "Each of you must repent of your sins and turn to God and be baptized in the name of Jesus Christ for the forgiveness of your sins. Then you will receive the gift of the Holy Spirit."*

Acts 4:31 AMP *"And when they had prayed, the place where they were meeting together was shaken [a sign of God's presence]; and they were all filled with the Holy Spirit and began to speak the word of God with boldness and courage."*

Acts 8:14–17 AMP *"When the apostles in Jerusalem heard that [the people of] Samaria had accepted the word of God, they sent Peter and John to them.[15]They came down and prayed for them that they might receive the Holy Spirit; [16]for He had not yet fallen on any of them; they had simply been baptized in the name of the Lord Jesus [as His possession].[17]Then Peter and John laid their hands on them [one by one], and they received the Holy Spirit."*

Acts 10:44–48 NLT *"Even as Peter was saying these things, the Holy Spirit fell upon all who were listening to the message.[45]The Jewish believers who came with Peter were amazed that the gift of the Holy Spirit had been poured out on the Gentiles, too.[46]For they heard them speaking in other tongues and praising God. Then Peter asked,[47]"Can anyone object to their being baptized, now that they have received the Holy Spirit just as we did?"[48]So he gave orders for them to be baptized in the name of Jesus Christ. Afterward Cornelius asked him to stay with them for several days."*

Hebrews 2:4 NLT *"And God confirmed the message by giving signs and wonders and various miracles and gifts of the Holy Spirit whenever he chose."*

There is a lot to say about being baptized in the Holy Spirit, but the main point is to seek and ask to be filled. Concerning asking God to be baptized with the Holy Spirit, we don't have to be afraid or confused.

Luke 11:13 NASB *"So if you, despite being evil, know how to give good gifts to your children, how much more will your heavenly Father give the Holy Spirit to those who ask Him?"*

Jesus said in **Matthew 7:7 NIV** *"Ask and it will be given to you; seek and you will find; knock and the door will be opened to you."*

The Holy Spirit is a person. God has revealed Himself as God the Father, God the Son, and God the Holy Spirit—the Triune God. The Holy Spirit is the part of the "God-Head" that is here on earth, whereas the scriptures say that the Father and the Son are in heaven.

If we already had everything we needed, why would Jesus tell us to ask the Father to give us the Holy Spirit? Why would Jesus tell His disciples and followers to go to Jerusalem and "wait" to be baptized in the Holy Spirit (Acts 1:4, Luke 24:49)? Why would Paul when he went to Ephesus ask the new believers if they had received the Holy Spirit, when they had already believed and confessed Jesus as Lord (Acts 19:1-2)?

Jesus told His disciples to wait to be baptized in the Holy Spirit before they did anything else, which should establish the matter right there. Remember, most of what we do with our faith—to follow Jesus—is summed up in one word: obedience.

Jesus even said it was to our advantage that He would physically leave us here on earth, go to the Father, and then send us the Holy Spirit (John 16:7, 28). Many would say that having Jesus here with us in the flesh would be better, but why did Jesus say it was better if He left and then sent the Holy Spirit?

Jesus, while here on earth, was in the flesh just like us and was limited to being in one location at a time. Jesus coming in the flesh was necessary to die in our place (Romans 5:15–17). But once Jesus had paid the price for our sin, God's plan was to send the Holy Spirit, who is not constrained by one human body and can now be in every believer. Think of how amazing that really is, and let it sink in for a minute. God has chosen to live inside those who believe in Him through the person of the Holy Spirit.

Many get caught up in debating whether the gifts of the Holy Spirit are for today. First, I will restate that the Holy Spirit is a person, and to be baptized means to be submerged. When you first believe you are saved and receive what is called the "sure deposit of your salvation" (Ephesians 1:13–14). What Jesus was telling His disciples was that they needed to be submerged in the Holy Spirit and empowered. This is recorded as a separate experience multiple times in the Book of Acts.

Concerning the gifts of the Holy Spirit:

1 Corinthians 12:4–11 NASB *"Now there are varieties of gifts, but the same Spirit. ⁵And there are varieties of ministries, and the same Lord. ⁶There are varieties of effects, but the same God who works all things in all persons. ⁷But to each one is given the manifestation of the Spirit for the common good. ⁸For to one is given the word of wisdom through the Spirit, and to another the word of knowledge according to the same Spirit; ⁹to another faith by the same Spirit, and to another gifts of healing by the one Spirit, ¹⁰and to another the effecting of miracles, and to another prophecy, and to another the distinguishing of spirits, to another various kinds of tongues, and to another the interpretation of tongues. ¹¹But one and the same Spirit works all these things, distributing to each one individually just as He wills."*

The gifts of the Holy Spirit are tools that help us fulfill our purpose and destiny within God's kingdom here on earth. Gifts are gifts, and we should receive them with thanksgiving. When we are "face-to-face" with Jesus and in heaven, we will no longer need these gifts or be empowered to be witnesses. When we are "face-to-face" with Jesus, we will know everything we need to know, but for now, we know in part and prophesy in part.

1 Corinthians 13:12 NASB *"For now we see in a mirror dimly, but then face to face; now I know in part, but then I will know fully, just as I also have been fully known."*

Some say the gifts were taken away or ceased. Let's at least consider this thought for argument's sake. There were the Old Testament covenant(s), and now there is the New Testament covenant established through the death and resurrection of Jesus. There is not a "new-new" covenant whereby God said salvation and forgiveness of sins are still available, but I'm taking back my Holy Spirit and the gifts I gave you. God didn't say, "I just gave you the gifts upfront until we could get the Bible out in print or until the Apostles die."

Jesus knew that we would need all the help we could get. You can't take away the weapons and resources from your armed forces and expect them to win. We are truly in a war and need the Holy Spirit and the empowerment of the Holy Spirit if we are going to win this war and endure to the end.

Ephesians 6:12 NASB *"For our struggle is not against flesh and blood, but against the rulers, against the powers, against the* *world forces of this darkness, against the spiritual forces of wickedness in the heavenly places."*

Another note is that the gifts aren't just for believers but serve as a witness to unbelievers that they will be convicted of sin (1 Corinthians 14:22–25).

And it's not just about gifts; we are talking about the presence of God within us and flowing through us. Notice how John 7:38 says, "Whoever believes in me." And says, those who believe "were later to receive." Just like salvation itself, where you must step out in faith, in Luke 11:13, Jesus said that the Father will give the Holy Spirit to those who ask Him.

John 7:38–39 NIV *"Whoever believes in me, as Scripture has said, rivers of living water will flow from within them." ^{39} By this he meant the Spirit, whom those who believed in him were later to receive. Up to that time the Spirit had not been given, since Jesus had not yet been glorified."*

There is one Scripture that gets taken out of context by some but be careful when establishing a doctrine on just one scripture. Any one Scripture can be taken out of context and then misinterpreted. It was and still is imperative for the growth and survival of the church that we are a Spirit-filled body of believers. So, what is the Scripture that some have misinterpreted?

1 Corinthians 13:8–9 NASB *"Love never fails; but if there are gifts of prophecy, they will be done away with; if there are tongues, they will cease; if there is knowledge, it will be done away* *with.⁹For we know in part and prophesy in part; ¹⁰but when the perfect comes, the partial will be done away with."*

The follow-up to this is in **1 Corinthians 13:12 AMP**
"For now [in this time of imperfection] we see in a mirror dimly [a blurred reflection, a riddle, an enigma], but then [when the time of perfection comes, we will see reality] face to face. Now I know in part [just in fragments], but then I will know fully, just as I have been fully known [by God]."

If we read 1 Corinthians 13 in context, it doesn't say that we don't speak in tongues or prophesy or that we don't have faith in miracles, but it does say that having these gifts and using them without love is meaningless. Paul is saying the gifts are not the point, but he doesn't say they aren't important. What Paul does say is:

1 Corinthians 12:31 NASB *"But earnestly desire the greater gifts."*

To be clear, we are still in the "time" of imperfection and are not "face to face" with Jesus yet. Until God's will "is" done on earth as it is in heaven, we have not arrived at any realm of perfection. Remember, the gifts are just tools. God gives the gifts as He chooses.

1 Corinthians 12:11 AMP *"All these things [the gifts, the achievements, the abilities, the empowering] are brought about by one and the same [Holy] Spirit, distributing to each one individually just as He chooses."*

In the book of Acts, on the day of Pentecost, Peter quotes a prophecy from the book of Joel.

Acts 2:16–18 NIV

"No, this is what was spoken by the prophet Joel:
[17]In the last days, God says,
I will pour out my Spirit on all people.
Your sons and daughters will prophesy,
your young men will see visions,
your old men will dream dreams.
[18]Even on my servants, both men and women,
I will pour out my Spirit in those days,
and they will prophesy."

My encouragement is for you to seek whatever God has for you. Ask God to empower you by His Holy Spirit, to fill you, and to baptize you; so that you have everything you need to fulfill your destiny in Christ Jesus.

BE CONNECTED

It is important to be around other believers.

Hebrews 10:25 NLT *"And let us not neglect our meeting together, as some people do, but encourage one another, especially now that the day of his return is drawing near."*

If you are standing alone, you are an easy target for the enemy. Yes, you have an enemy called the devil or Satan.

1 Peter 5:8 NASB *"Be of sober spirit, be on the alert. Your adversary, the devil, prowls around like a roaring lion, seeking someone to devour."*

But don't be overconcerned either, because the scriptures say in **1 John 4:4 NASB** *"You are from God, little children, and have overcome them; because greater is He who is in you than he who is in the world."*

James 4:7 NASB *says, "Submit therefore to God. But resist the devil, and he will flee from you."*

You need to have fellowship with other believers. You will be influenced by those you surround yourself with.

Proverbs 13:20 NASB *"One who walks with wise people will be wise, but a companion of fools will suffer harm."*

Proverbs 27:17 NIV *"As iron sharpens iron, so one person sharpens another."*

It is imperative that believers help each other, encourage, pray for, lift up, and bear each other's burdens.

Galatians 6:2 AMP *"Carry one another's burdens and in this way, you will fulfill the requirements of the law of Christ [that is, the law of Christian love]."*

1 Thessalonians 5:11 NIV *"Therefore encourage one another and build each other up, just as in fact you are doing."*

There is also power in corporate prayer.

James 5:16 NIV *"Therefore confess your sins to each other and pray for each other so that you may be healed. The prayer of a righteous person is powerful and effective."*

Matthew 18:19–20 NIV *"Again, truly I tell you that if two of you on earth agree about anything they ask for, it will be done for them by my Father in heaven.²⁰For where two or three gather in my name, there am I with them."*

We need to take time for personal prayer, reading the Word and worship, as well as corporately praying, worshiping, taking communion, giving testimonies, sharing, and hearing the Word of God. There is a model from the early church documented in the Book of Acts that is worth copying.

Acts 2:42 NASB *"They were continually devoting themselves to the apostles' teaching and to fellowship, to the breaking of bread and to prayer."*

Remember, we are the body of Christ being built together.

1 Peter 2:5 NLT *"And you are living stones that God is building into his spiritual temple. What's more, you are his holy priests. Through the mediation of Jesus Christ, you offer spiritual sacrifices that please God."*

Ephesians 2:19-22 NASB *"So then you are no longer strangers and foreigners, but you are fellow citizens with the saints, and are of God's household,[20] having been built on the foundation of the apostles and prophets, Christ Jesus Himself being the cornerstone,[21] in whom the whole building, being fitted together, is growing into a holy temple in the Lord,[22] in whom you also are being built together into a dwelling of God in the Spirit."*

Every believer has a place and a purpose in the body of Christ.

> We need to take time for personal prayer, reading the Word and worship as well as corporately praying, worshiping, taking communion, giving testimonies, sharing, and hearing the Word of God.

PRAYER

The Greek word for "to pray" is proseuchomai. The definition in the Strong's Concordance is simply to pray. Under the word study, it says, "properly, to exchange wishes; *pray*—*literally*, to *interact with* the Lord by switching human *wishes* (ideas) for *His wishes* as He imparts faith ('divine *persuasion*')."

Prayer is more than just asking God for things you want or need; it's an ongoing conversation with God. Think of what an honor it is that the creator of the universe wants to communicate with us and have a personal relationship with us. Know that prayer is a two-way conversation. You can speak to God but take time in His presence to listen. For me, I like to write my prayers and then write what I hear God saying to me. You will know it's God if it lines up with His written Word. If it doesn't line up with God's written Word, then that's not God. What a privilege it is to be able to approach God and hear His voice.

1 Timothy 2:5 NASB *"For there is one God, and one mediator also between God and mankind, the man Christ Jesus."*

When Jesus died and rose again, the veil of the temple was torn, and direct access to the Holy of Holies was made available to every believer. We don't have to go to a priest or pastor to pray on our behalf.

Matthew 27:51 AMP *"And [at once] the veil [of the Holy of Holies] of the temple was torn in two from top to bottom; the earth shook, and the rocks were split apart."*

It is important to seek God daily. Having an ongoing conversation with God is part of your relationship with Him. The Lord's Prayer, found in Luke chapter 11, was a prayer that Jesus taught His disciples. Here is a breakdown of that prayer; you can use it as a model.

Approaching the throne of God: *Our Father who art in Heaven.* This is simply identifying who we are praying to.

Worship: *Hallowed be thy name*—to worship means to create an expression of honor or to attribute worth to the object of worship. This statement honors God's name and acknowledges that God is worthy, God is holy, righteous, just, our creator, our Father, etc.

Intercessory prayer: *Your kingdom come; your will be done, on earth as it is in heaven.* Here, you can pray for exactly what it says: "God's will to be done." Ask for anything according to God's will, and you will have it (1 John 5:14). Why would Jesus say to pray for God's will to be done? If God is sovereign, isn't God's will already being done? The best way I can explain it is that man has free will; we live in a fallen world, and God's will is not always being done on earth.

When God's will was not done in heaven, Lucifer, one of the archangels, along with the angels that rebelled with him, were cast out. Sometimes, God's will is being done on earth, but we need to pray for God's will to be done on earth and in our lives daily.

You can pray, "God, may Your will be done in my life. Show me what You want me to do and empower me to accomplish whatever that is. Give me eyes to see things the way You see them and ears to hear so that I might know Your will for my life. I pray Your will be done in my family, at my work, in my neighborhood, in my church, in my state, in the government, and in the world.

I pray for salvation for the lost, as your Word says that You wish for none to perish but for all to come to repentance. If You be lifted up that You would draw all men unto Yourself."

Prayer of petition: *Give us this day our daily bread.* This is praying for our physical, spiritual, and mental needs to be met. "Thank you, God, for providing all of my needs according to Your riches in glory. I ask for favor in time, money, and relationships; for peace that passes all understanding, wisdom, knowledge, focus, clarity, grace, mercy, strength, courage, boldness, discernment, influence, and opportunities."

Confession, repentance, forgiveness: *And forgive us our debts, as we also have forgiven our debtors.* "God forgive me of my sin, whether in thought, deed, or lack of deed. I forgive those who have sinned against me and hold nothing against anyone. I forgive myself. Thank you for dying on the cross on my behalf and paying the price for my sin. I receive your gift of salvation, which cancels the debt of my sin. Thank you for forgiveness, that You blot out my sins and do not count them against me, that You cast my sin as far as the east is from the west."

Spiritual warfare or protection: *And lead us not into temptation but deliver us from the evil one.* "I put on the belt of truth. May the truth of Your Word be ever present in my day and set me free from anything false or any bondage. I put on the breastplate of righteousness. Thank you, Your Word says that I am the righteousness of God in Christ Jesus. Thank you that I am in right standing with You because of what You did. May this breastplate guard my heart, and may I be wise in what I look at and do. I put on the shoes of the gospel of peace. May I bring the good news of salvation in love to a lost and dying world.

I put on the helmet of salvation. May I take every thought captive to the obedience of the Lord Jesus and cast down vain imaginations and every high thing that exalts itself against the knowledge of God. I take up the shield of faith. May faith surround me as a shield and protect me from the attacks of the enemy. I take up the sword of the Spirit, Your Word, may it be both defensive and offensive, to battle the enemy.

May I hide your Word in my heart and mind so that I will not sin against You."

Praise and Worship: *For yours is the kingdom, the power, and the glory forever,* "Amen" (so be it or let it be done).

SAVED BY FAITH

- If you have never put your faith in Jesus and accepted the sacrifice Jesus made on the cross for you personally.

- If you have never repented and confessed Jesus as your Lord.

- If, after learning more about what it means to put your faith in Jesus Christ as Lord, and want to make a confession with understanding.

Let's take a moment and offer up a prayer together.

Father God,

Thank you for sending Your Son, Jesus, to die on the cross on my behalf. I acknowledge that Jesus was the only one qualified to pay the price for my sin. I acknowledge that there is no other name under heaven by which I can be saved. I believe Jesus Christ is the Son of God, God the Son, the Messiah, and the holy Lamb that was slain before the foundation of the world. I believe Jesus was conceived by the Holy Spirit and born of a virgin. I believe that Jesus came and lived a sinless life in the flesh. I believe in the life, death, and resurrection of Jesus. I repent. I confess that I have sinned and violated your laws. I ask for forgiveness for my sin. I understand that the wages of sin is death and that I cannot pay this debt on my own behalf. Only through Jesus's death and His blood being shed could my sin be covered, my debt paid, and Your wrath be satisfied against my sin. Thank you, God, for paying the price for my sin and for the blood of Jesus that cleanses me from all unrighteousness. Thank you, Father, for raising Jesus from the dead. I confess Jesus as Lord. Jesus is my Lord. I give you everything that I am and submit my will to You and the Lordship of Jesus Christ. Thank you that Jesus is now my Savior and that I am saved. Thank you for writing my name in the Lamb's Book of Life. Thank you that Your Word says that as many as believe, You gave them the right to be called children of God. I will live my life for You from this day forward. I am a new creation in Christ. I am a child of God. I give You thanks and praise. In Jesus name, Amen.

If you prayed that prayer for the first time, welcome to your new life in Christ. If you recommitted your life to Christ, God receives you back with open arms.

We covered God's plan of redemption for His creation throughout this book. I like to call this plan of redemption a package deal. Remember, in Acts 2:38, Peter said to repent and be baptized, and you will receive the gift of the Holy Spirit. Don't stop with just praying a prayer. Don't stop after being water-baptized. Don't even stop after being filled with the Holy Spirit. Your walk with God is daily, and it's for eternity. We get to start this walk with God from the moment we believe, repent, confess, and surrender.

I will leave you with this one last Scripture from the Amplified translation.

Romans 8:28 AMP *"And we know [with great confidence] that God [who is deeply concerned about us] causes all things to work together [as a plan] for good for those who love God to those who are called according to His plan and purpose."*

May your journey be filled with awe and wonder as you follow and serve the one true living God.

References:

Scripture taken from the NEW AMERICAN STANDARD BIBLE, Copyright © 1960, 1971, 1977, 1995, 2020 by The Lockman Foundation. All rights reserved. Used with permission: www.Lockman.org

Scripture quotations are taken from the Amplified® Bible (AMP), Copyright © 2015 by The Lockman Foundation. Used by permission. www.Lockman.org

New Living Translation (NLT) *HOLY BIBLE*, New Living Translation, copyright © 1996, 2004, 2015 by Tyndale House Foundation. Used by permission of Tyndale House Publishers, Inc., Carol Stream, Illinois 60188. All rights reserved.

Scripture quotations marked (NIV) are taken from the Holy Bible, New International Version®, NIV®. Copyright © 1973, 1978, 1984, 2011 by Biblica, Inc.™ Used by permission of Zondervan. All rights reserved worldwide. www.Zondervan.com The "NIV" and "New International Version" are trademarks registered in the United States Patent and Trademark Office by Biblica, Inc.™

Miracles Today, Craig S. Keener, Baker Academic, a division of Baker Publishing Group

Strong's Exhaustive Concordance of the Bible was used for all Greek word references. Copyright 1995 by Thomas Nelson Publishers.

Article by Fellowship of Israel Related Ministries

ABOUT THE AUTHOR

Matthew L. Adrianson was born in 1970 in Zeeland, Michigan, and grew up in Jenison, Michigan. Growing up in church, but maybe a little different than some. Over the years, his family attended several different churches of various denominations.

Matthew's faith has always been a vital part of his life. The first church he remembers attending was a Baptist church when he was five years old. One of his clearest and most vivid childhood memories happened at that same age. He remembers praying with his mother at their kitchen table and receiving Jesus into his life.

At some point, he remembers going to a Reformed church, and then, at age 12, after his mother got a job as a choir director, they attended a United Brethren church. While attending the United Brethren church, Matthew was water baptized and confessed Jesus as Lord in a public setting. Around 1984, his family started attending an Assemblies of God church in Wyoming, Michigan. This was the first church where he consistently served by playing drums.

Matthew graduated from Grand Valley State University in Allendale, Michigan, in 1992 with a bachelor's degree in music.

In the summer of 1993, he did a three-month tour with a group called "The Celebrant Singers," based out of Visalia, California. This tour included a segment traveling to Bulgaria and then back to the United States. One of the unique components of this ministry is that it consisted of both Protestants and Catholics. The concerts were performed in both Protestant and Catholic churches, giving Matthew a broader view of those professing to be Christians. The group played concerts every night and included testimonies, praying for the sick, the hurting, and the broken, as well as witnessing to the lost. This trip had a major impact on him and played a significant role in forming his worldview.

After that tour, Matthew started writing songs, putting a band together, and performing concerts in churches in Michigan. In 1994, there was an opportunity to go to Russia with another local artist, Randy Bouwer, and remembers playing on a Sunday morning with a Russian praise band in Moscow.

From 1997 to 2007, Matthew played drums at Resurrection Life Church in Grandville, Michigan. During his ten years at Resurrection Life, he was blessed to be on five music albums, playing drums and percussion. He played under the leadership of Curt Coffield, Michael Gungor, and Ken Reynolds.

Matthew currently resides in West Michigan and is focusing on writing and recording original music. He is actively taking leadership training and ministry classes through City Church Rockford in Michigan, as well as Bible courses through Global University.

The inspiration to write this book included his desire for everyone to truly know Jesus as their Lord and Savior!

www.ingramcontent.com/pod-product-compliance
Lightning Source LLC
Chambersburg PA
CBHW071826020426
42331CB00007B/1620